FAVORITE FAIRY TALES
Coloring Book

Fran Newman-D'Amico

DOVER PUBLICATIONS, INC.
Mineola, New York

Get ready to take a trip to the world of make-believe! Inside this book you'll find thirty kid-friendly, ready-to-color illustrations featuring your favorite fairy tale characters. Use your imagination to add your own artistic touch to The Little Mermaid, Puss in Boots, Little Red Riding Hood, Sleeping Beauty, and more.

Copyright

Copyright © 2004, 2013 by Dover Publications, Inc.
All rights reserved.

Bibliographical Note

BOOST Favorite Fairy Tales Coloring Book first published by Dover Publications, Inc., in 2013, is a revised edition of *Favorite Fairy Tales Coloring Book,* originally published by Dover in 2004.

International Standard Book Number
ISBN-13: 978-0-486-49403-6
ISBN-10: 0-486-49403-9

Manufactured in the United States by LSC Communications
49403907   2020
www.doverpublications.com

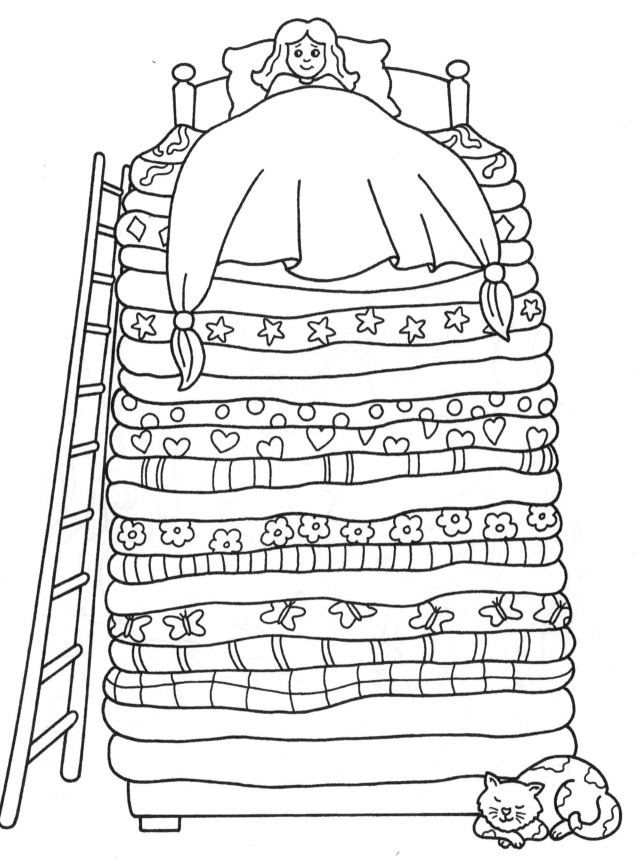

The Princess and the Pea

Not even twenty mattresses could make the princess happy.

 RL.K.1 With prompting and support, ask and answer questions about key details in a text. Also **RL.K.7; RF.K.1; SL.K.1.**

The Little Mermaid

The little mermaid loved her friends.

 RL.K.7 With prompting and support, describe the relationship between illustrations and the story in which they appear. Also **RF.K.1; SL.K.2.**

Jack and the Beanstalk

Jack climbed and climbed and climbed till at last he reached the sky.

 RL.K.1 With prompting and support, ask and answer questions about key details in a text. Also **RL.K.7; RF.K.1, RF.K.2.**

Thumbelina

Thumbelina soared above the mountains.

 RL.K.7 With prompting and support, describe the relationship between illustrations and the story in which they appear. Also **RF.K.1; SL.K.3; L.K.1.**

Rapunzel

Rapunzel let down her long golden hair.

 RL.K.1 With prompting and support, ask and answer questions about key details in a text. Also **RL.K.5, RL.K.7; RF.K.1.**

The Three Little Pigs

The wolf looked on as the three little pigs danced and sang.

 RL.K.7 With prompting and support, describe the relationship between illustrations and the story in which they appear. Also **RL.K.10; RF.K.1.**

Puss in Boots

The cat had in his bag a rabbit for the king.

Pinocchio

Pinocchio was a wooden puppet that longed to be a boy.

 RL.K.7 With prompting and support, describe the relationship between illustrations and the story in which they appear. Also **RL.K.10; RF.K.1; SL.K.1; L.K.1.**

The Butterfly

Butterfly couldn't decide which flower to choose for his bride.

 RL.K.1 With prompting and support, ask and answer questions about key details in a text. Also **RL.K.7; RF.K.1.a, RF.K.1.c.**

The Elves and the Shoemaker

The elves made a new pair of shoes in a flash.

 CCSS **RL.K.7** With prompting and support, describe the relationship between illustrations and the story in which they appear. Also **RL.K.10; RF.K.1; SL.K.1.**

The Nightingale

His song was the sweetest sound near and far.

 RL.K.1 With prompting and support, ask and answer questions about key details in a text. Also **RL.K.5, RL.K.7; RF.K.1, RF.K.4; SL.K.2.**

The Frog Prince

The frog told the princess he would help her get her ball.

 RL.K.3 With prompting and support, identify characters, settings, and major events in a story. Also **RL.K.7; SL.K.1.**

The Ugly Duckling

The ugly duckling knew he didn't fit in.

 RL.K.1 With prompting and support, ask and answer questions about key details in a text.
Also **RL.K.7; RF.K.1, RF.K.4; SL.K.1.**

Little Red Riding Hood

She picked some flowers to bring to her grandmother's house.

 RL.K.5 Recognize common types of texts (e.g., storybooks, poems). Also **RL.K.7, RL.K.10; RF.K.1.**

Beauty and the Beast

Every day the Beast asked Beauty to marry him.

Snow White

She saw wild animals, but they did her no harm.

 RL.K.7 With prompting and support, describe the relationship between illustrations and the story in which they appear. Also **RL.K.10; RF.K.1; SL.K.2.**

Hansel and Gretel

They came to a house made of candy and sugar.

 RL.K.1 With prompting and support, ask and answer questions about key details in a text. Also **RL.K.7; RF.K.1; SL.K.1.**

The Golden Goose

When he cut down the tree he found a goose with feathers of pure gold.

The Brave Little Tailor

He knocked down seven flies with a single blow.

 RL.K.1 With prompting and support, ask and answer questions about key details in a text. Also **RL.K.5, RL.K.7; RF.K.1.**

The Fisherman and His Wife

"I'm not really a flounder, but an enchanted prince."

The Red Shoes

She danced over field and meadow, in sunshine and in rain.

Sleeping Beauty

The princess fell into a deep sleep, which lasted 100 years.

 RL.K.1 With prompting and support, ask and answer questions about key details in a text. Also **RL.K.7; RF.K.1; SL.K.1.**

The Bremen Town Musicians

They screeched, meowed, howled, and brayed as loudly as they could.

 RL.K.4 Ask and answer questions about unknown words in a text. Also **RL.K.7, RL.K.10; RF.K.1.**

Tom Thumb

He was wise and nimble but never grew larger than a thumb.

 RL.K.1 With prompting and support, ask and answer questions about key details in a text. Also **RL.K.4, RL.K.7; RF.K.1; L.K.6.**

The Goose Girl

The real princess was forced to tend to the king's geese.

RL.K.1 With prompting and support, ask and answer questions about key details in a text. Also **RL.K.7; RF.K.1; SL.K.1.**

The Six Swans

The six shirts were ready, and now the young queen could smile.

CCSS **RL.K.7** With prompting and support, describe the relationship between illustrations and the story in which they appear. Also **RL.K.10; RF.K.1; SL.K.1; L.K.1.**

Cinderella

After she had put on the silver dress, she was as beautiful as a rose washed in dew.

 RL.K.1 With prompting and support, ask and answer questions about key details in a text. Also **RL.K.4, RL.K.7; RF.K.1; SL.K.3; L.K.4.**

The Cat and the Fox

The fox had a whole bag of tricks, but the cat had only one.

 RL.K.7 With prompting and support, describe the relationship between illustrations and the story in which they appear. Also **RL.K.10; RF.K.1; L.K.1.**

Goldilocks and the Three Bears

The porridge in the smallest bowl was just right, and she ate it all up.

 RL.K.1 With prompting and support, ask and answer questions about key details in a text. Also **RL.K.7; RF.K.1; L.K.6.**

Rumpelstiltskin

The strange little man spun all the straw into gold.

 RL.K.1 With prompting and support, ask and answer questions about key details in a text. Also **RL.K.7; RF.K.1; SL.K.1.**